Angels
in Afghanistan

by Joseph R. Perez Jr

DORRANCE
PUBLISHING CO
EST. 1920
PITTSBURGH, PENNSYLVANIA 15238

Dorrance Publishing Co
585 Alpha Drive
Pittsburgh, PA 15238
Visit our website at *www.dorrancebookstore.com*

ISBN: 978-1-6393-7164-8
ESIBN: 978-1-6393-7975-0

Angels
in Afghanistan

CHAPTER ONE
Joining the Military

"For he shall give his angels charge over thee, to keep thee in all thy ways."

Psalm 91:11

There were two big moments in my life: accepting Christ as my savior when I was thirteen years old, and joining the military. Although they seem unrelated, the first experience would turn out to have a big impact on the second.

We were living in Lynnwood, Washington during the summer of 2003. It was June, and I had just turned thirteen. I remember it was hot that day, my elbows were sticking to the warm surface of the dining room table. My brother came to where I was sitting and handed me a pamphlet, he said, "You need to accept Christ as your savior."

I have always believed in God. Some might say I'm a bit too trusting (even gullible), but when it came to God, I didn't question Him, the same way I wouldn't question someone's authority. I thought, *who are we to challenge Him?*

It's hard to explain, but I had an overwhelming feeling, a sense that this was something I needed to do. I left the dining room and walked upstairs to my bedroom. Sitting on the edge of the bed, I flipped over the pamphlet; there was a small prayer on the back. With

1

tears rolling down my cheeks, I began to recite it. "Dear Jesus, I know I'm a sinner, and I know I've done wrong, I trust you today, and only you to take me to heaven when I die."

As I said the words out loud, I accepted Christ as my savior. I had known Him as a savior, as The Savior, but never as my savior. That day everything changed.

I felt an overwhelming presence. It was very emotional. As if a yoke had been lifted off me, I felt weightless. I remember walking downstairs and standing by the front door, and having almost an out of body experience. I felt two angels dressed in white lift me out of my body and carry me outside. I was flying high above the neighborhood, and I could see everything below me.

This wasn't the first time I'd had extra sensory perception. From a young age I could sometimes feel things, you could say they were of a spiritual nature. It was fleeting and hard to describe, but sometimes I could detect a presence, something standing near me, trying to get into my mind. I would freak my mother out by calling her into the room and saying, "There's something in here with me." I'm not sure if she believed me, but she always checked. This out of body experience was like nothing I'd ever felt before. I felt free.

Before this incident, I had attended Catholic Church, but I wasn't encouraged to read the Bible or have a personal relationship with Christ. This was all brand new to me. After this happened, I couldn't put the Bible down; I went to an independent fundamentalist Baptist Church, I prayed, I wrote sermons. I had so many questions that needed to be answered. More importantly, I wanted to tell everyone about Christ.

I had two older sisters and one older brother, which made me the baby of the family. My parents split when I was very young and I grew up in two places. I stayed with my mom in the summer, and during the school year I lived with my dad in Germany where he was stationed in the military. For me it was simple: When I lived with my mom, I listened to her, and when I lived with my dad, I listened to him. My older brother lived full time with our mom, so the separation was hard and we weren't as close as we could have been. Regardless, I looked up to him.

In 2003, my father moved us from Southern Bavaria to Stuttgart, and I stayed there until I graduated from high school. After high school, I set my sights on college and got accepted to Pacific Lutheran University in Tacoma, Washington on a four-year scholarship through the Army ROTC program. Originally, my major was political science and international relations, and my plan was to go to law school after college through an Army education delay program to be a lawyer in the military. By my junior year I started thinking about joining the military first, and then going to law school after.

All ROTC college students are required to attend a nationwide leadership training and performance evaluation; the Leadership Development Assessment Course (LDAC). At the end of the four-week program each of the students is ranked from 1 to 6,000, and assessed for which branch of the military they'd be assigned—whether that was infantry, medical, finance, intel or whichever specific branch in the Army. We spent the entire time on the military base in Fort Lewis, Washington, and by the end of it, I definitely felt like this was where I needed to be.

After returning to college from training, we had to select our final preferences on our branches. On the last day, I was sitting in my dorm room thinking hard about my future. Originally, I had chosen military intelligence as the branch of the military I'd like to go into. Suddenly, I got a strong intuition to change my preferences.

It was after 5 P.M. on a Friday night and I was sure nobody would be in the ROTC office of Memorial Gym, but I took a chance and decided to walk over there anyway. Memorial Gym was the oldest, most run-down building on campus. Standing in front, everything was dark, and I couldn't really tell if anyone was inside. I reached out for the door handle expecting it to be locked, but instead it was open.

Looking around the dark hallway, I thought, *nobody is here anyway.* I decided to go check it out.

The senior commander's office was towards the left of the entrance, so I took a left turn down the hall and headed that way. Again, I was totally shocked when I saw light coming from his office. I found Lieutenant Colonel Jason Schrader sitting at his desk, alone.

He looked up when he saw me. Let me stress that this was a highly unusual move on my part—in the military, you're never supposed to skip the chain of command—so I was taking a huge risk. Schrader was soft spoken, professional, and intelligent. He never yelled, but he meant business, and I had a lot of respect for him.

I said, "I know that nobody is supposed to be here, sir, and this is a long shot...but today is the last day to change our selection and I was wondering if there's any way I can change mine to infantry."

I was expecting him to say—it's too late, the staff is all gone, nobody is working. Instead, he picked up the phone and dialed the HR director at home. He said, "I have a Joseph Perez here in my office, and I need you to change his preferences to infantry right now."

I thanked him, and left. A few months later, I received my official assessment and my ranking. They had determined I was most suited to go into the infantry—the same area I'd chosen.

There are no accidents, and this was too much of a coincidence. To me, it was a sign.

Going to Ranger School

> "You will reach your breaking point, don't let it be your failing point."
>
> – D.M.

In the book *Where Men Win Glory*, Pat Tillman, the former NFL player writes about enlisting in the United States Army Ranger Battalion (special operations) and going to Ranger School after turning down a once in a lifetime football contract. There is one particular quote that stood out to me as I read this book, "There were some times when I just thought I wasn't going to make it."

I didn't know anything about Ranger School except for what I'd heard and read. I thought, *if a pro NFL athlete didn't think he was going to make it—how am I supposed to make it?*

We were in Fort Benning, Georgia, and everybody was watching videos about Ranger School and preparing themselves. I didn't want to psych myself out, so I went back to the assigned housing area on post and started putting my packing list together. I wasn't sure exactly what I was getting myself into, but I knew I was going to try to do my best no matter what.

Ranger School is split up into four phases: RAP Week, Benning Phase, Mountain Phase, and Florida Phase. The first phase, RAP week, is the one that the public is the most familiar with, it's where all the physical fitness tests are. You get smoked a lot and there's multiple obstacle courses, a twelve-mile march, and combat tests. You basically do a lot of physical activity, and there's not a lot of sleep. During this phase, most of the new recruits drop out. But if you pass, you go into the next phase, Benning Phase, where you are part of a small unit, practicing tactics at a squad level. After you pass that, you go to Dahlonega, Georgia for Mountain Phase. This was the part of Ranger School that took the most toll on my body.

Mountain Phase consists of foot patrols carrying a fifty-plus-pound pack on your back. Typically, you're in so much pain, you can't focus on anything except taking the next step. I learned to zero in on the nearest tree up ahead of me, walk to that tree, lean on it for a break, and then find the next tree to focus on. That way I didn't have to look at the steep incline we were walking up. It was all I could do.

Everyone that's made it this far in Ranger School remembers the blueberry pancakes in the dining hall. After hours of brutal climbing and walking patrols, they'd give us three to four minutes to eat. Even though you only have those pancakes on your lips for a few seconds before they start yelling at you to start moving again, it's the best tasting thing ever. We'd only get two or three hours to sleep and eat per night, and there was fire-guard, so I was averaging roughly an hour and a half of sleep each night, tops. I remember being more exhausted than I'd ever been in my life. Many times, I'd skip eating just so I could get a few extra seconds of sleep. Did you want to be a hungry ranger or a sleepy ranger? That was the perpetual question on our minds. Unfortunately, you can only skip meals so long before that starts to become a problem.

One night I found a package of Twizzlers in the mountains and I grabbed them and shoved them in my mouth. It was so awesome, these red cherry flavored Twizzlers, but they tasted crunchy and dry. Confused, I stopped chewing. *Why do they taste like this?* Suddenly I heard one of my mates say, "Hey! What are you doing?" I stood up. *What the heck?* There were bunches of dry leaves in my mouth—I had been hallucinating. I tried to spit them out, but my mouth was dry and parched and I had the taste of those leaves in my mouth for hours. I was so disgusted and embarrassed.

Before going to Ranger School, a friend of mine told me, "You're going to reach your breaking point, but don't let it be your failing point." Mountain Phase was brutal, but at the end they'd told me I had passed and would be headed to Florida Phase.

By the time we got to Florida Phase, we were on Eglin Airforce base practicing platoon level tactics. Another name for Florida Phase is Swamp Phase, and I quickly learned why. We were walking through mud and water at all times. I had heat exhaustion, I was in so much pain at times I felt like I was walking on nails. One day, I remember looking at the road trying to walk straight, but I had no control over my body. My limbs felt like rubber. They called me in, and told everybody to stop and go to the side. Before collapsing by the side of the road, in the mud, unconscious, I thought, *this is the moment he was talking about. There's no way I can make it through this.* And yet I did. There was a moment when I couldn't keep moving, I felt like I was overheating, could barely take any steps, and decided I was going to try, or die trying.

At this point, I had no idea whether I was passing or failing. Every time you go through to the next level, you are assessed for a leadership role, you either get a "go" or a "no go," to move onto the next phase. The only way you can know if you've passed is when you get put into a supporting leadership role, an indication you no longer need to be assessed and were given a go on your first attempt.

At the end of the Florida Phase, they took us aside and split us into two groups. With stern looks on their faces, they gave us the bad news that our group didn't pass and we would be retrained. I remember I wanted to break down and cry when I heard that. I just couldn't physically do it again. I looked at my friend, "What the heck?"

Then they smiled. "We're just kidding. You all passed."

The guys erupted into cheers and laughter, I jumped on my friend's back, I was so happy. What a relief.

Sixty-one days of Ranger School, and I graduated with my class, June 21st, 2013. It was a really good day. The only hard part was watching the ones who didn't pass stay behind as we got on the bus to go home. (This was really hard because I wanted them to pass, and you build strong relationships over the course.) Mostly, I was glad it was all over with. The next nine months I spent trying to recover and get myself physically back to where I was before Ranger School. Many times I'd go to the gym and my body just couldn't do anything. Not even a single push up. I ate anything I could get my hands on, I slept as much as possible.

This experience was the most spiritually empowering, but also the most emotionally and physically difficult thing I've ever done.

A friend once told me, "Attending this school taught me your body can take a lot more than you think."

After graduating, I knew what he was talking about.

Happy Birthday Afghanistan

I arrived at my first unit in July 2013, and was told I was going to be a company commander for a rear detachment unit. So, I wouldn't deploy. Unlike the other junior officers who constantly talked about, "I have to get on a deployment," my goal was to do my best, not chase deployment. It wasn't that I didn't want to get deployed, but I was trying to learn to be a lieutenant first.

A few days later my superior said, "You're fired, you'll be a platoon leader."

I said, "What?!"

"Just kidding. Someone just quit, we need you to go to Alpha Company."

I said, "Yes, sir." I grabbed my stuff and headed to our headquarters building to in-process with the new unit. I was surprised to find out immediately upon getting there that we would be deploying to Afghanistan.

They told me, "We're scheduled to leave the second week in March, but don't worry, they never push the date back."

That turned out not to be true. Later, I found out we were leaving early. We departed for Afghanistan on March 6, 2014, one day before my twenty-fourth birthday.

This was my first deployment, I had no idea what to expect. I remember the hardest part was saying goodbye to my family. The night before we left, they all came out to Fort Carson in Colorado Springs. I hugged my mother tight, and my church prayed over me. My whole family was there, and this was the last time I'd see them for certain until I came back. Civilians weren't allowed in the building so after saying goodbye, we went inside the Company Operating Facility to gather our weapons and sensitive items, completed our account of all personnel and headed to the airfield to fly out.

Before we boarded I told my platoon sergeant, "The only thing I care about is that everyone comes home safe."

Once we got on the plane, I felt my nerves dissipate. We would be passing through Romania on our way to Afghanistan. I looked out of the window at the ground below us, and thought about what I might find on the other side of this flight. I wasn't really scared. Just like Ranger School, I was focused on doing the best I could. Sitting there on the plane, I closed my eyes and said a prayer, "God please help bring everyone home safe, and if there is anyone who doesn't come home, please let it be me and not anyone in the platoon."

I spent my twenty-fourth birthday on a flight to Afghanistan. It was a birthday I'd never forget.

CHAPTER TWO
Praise God

*"If I get kicked out for talking about my faith, at least
I will get kicked out for the right reasons."*
—Joseph Perez

Reaching beneath the seat, I took a small piece of paper and stuck it to the underside with some tape. Then, I moved to the next one and did the same until every seat in the military vehicle had one under it. Printed on each piece of paper were Psalm 91 and Psalm 23, some of my favorite Bible verses. When I was done, I tucked a Bible in my breast pocket and some laminated Bible verses I kept on me for every patrol.

This was our first time "leaving the wire," a term used for leaving the protected area of the military base compound. Taping the Bible verses was a small ritual, but it helped calm my nerves and I wanted everyone to stay safe.

I didn't care if anyone thought I was weird for doing this. Whenever I went to a new unit, I never hesitated to tell people about my faith. I always said, "If I get kicked out for talking about my faith, at least I will get kicked out for the right reasons."

Although we'd trained exclusively for this moment, nothing could have prepared me for the feeling of being exposed in a combat zone. We climbed into the vehicle, me and another platoon leader. I was in full kit for the first time down range, sitting on top of thousands of pounds of steel in a Military All-Terrain Vehicle, with an automatic machine gun. From my vantage point as the gunner, I could get to know the lay of the land, but also if we hit contact, I'd be the first person responsible for responding with weapons. This wasn't target practice, and we weren't shooting blanks. I immediately felt a sense of responsibility and the importance of knowing my way around the weaponry.

Our mission that day was to relieve the outgoing patrol unit who were getting ready to return home, and also to engage local leaders and introduce ourselves to the Afghan police commanders we'd be working closely with to deter the Taliban. Ultimately, our mission was to build trust with the Afghan population, which was especially crucial at that time, because of the upcoming presidential Afghan elections for Ashraf Ghani and Abdullah Abdullah. We would be responsible for securing voting centers that would allow the local towns to vote safely. Establishing trust and rapport was critical as this would be the first presidential election in Afghanistan where everyone had the opportunity to vote.

Leaving the military compound, I was immediately aware of a heightened sense of safety. We headed out onto Highway 7, the main highway that runs south to north near the border of Pakistan, just east of Kandahar Airfield. As I surveyed the terrain, everything seemed to be a threat or an IED—trash on the side of the road, children playing, trucks stacked with mattresses fifteen feet high—I couldn't tell what was normal and what wasn't. The land looked very much like a desert in Texas or New Mexico, but with landmarks that were distinctly foreign. For instance, directly north was a mountain range, divided by the highway, and towards the base of the mountain was a large visible sign made of rocks that said NO DRUGS in English. We nicknamed it NO DRUGS mountain, and everyone knew if you could see the sign, you were just east of the highway. We passed countless trees and grape rows, everything was brown, hard cracked desert earth, and it was hot. The sun pounded down on us mercilessly. I could feel the sweat rub against my skin, and I shifted uncomfortably under the crushing weight of the gear.

Up ahead was our first destination, we parked the trucks on the side of the road and got out. In Afghanistan, the houses had no roofs, and the commander's house was no exception, it had just four walls, reminiscent of a pueblo style home, made of brown cracked dirt. The entryway was usually a cut-out door, which sometimes had a cloth covering, but most of the time it didn't.

Several of the men beckoned us inside. The commanders wore traditional Afghan dress with dark skirts, long black beards, and scarves to keep the sun off their neck. The police wore blue uniforms and boots. We told them we had security guards with us—we nicknamed them our "guardian angels" since their one job was to pull security for us wherever we went—and gestured to the men who came with us. The commander nodded, and then reached behind his robe and grabbed something behind his back. It was a pistol.

We froze.

My men exchanged glances, waiting to see if he was going to point this gun at us or not. I braced for the worst. Turned out, he was just showing us his weapon and explaining his job to us as the head of the police.

Standing there, I remember being nervous, and unsure what to say. In the back of my mind the whole time, I was wondering how to keep my men safe while forging this alliance with the Afghani leaders. We had to be respectful of their culture and get to know the people and their families on a personal level first, no talking business right away. That's when I remembered some advice my father had given me when I explained our mission to him. He said, "Try to find common ground."

After a few minutes of silence, finally, I cleared my throat.

I said, "I'm Joseph, I'll be taking over this area. I hope we can work together. Let's keep this area safe."

The commanders seemed receptive.

I continued, "We may come from different places, but we can all agree that the safety of our children and our families is the most important thing. I want to work with you to secure a safe and promising future for all of us."

The men talked amongst themselves before responding. I could tell they were trying to read my physical and emotional demeanor. Hopefully, they could tell I really wanted to help and that I cared, not only about my people, but them as well.

I said, "Whatever I know I will let you know, as long as you do the same for me. I value the lives of my men more than my own."

They agreed to this.

They motioned for us to sit down on some blankets on the floor, which was customary in Afghani culture. I put my weapon to the side, and sat next to my platoon sergeant. They gave us hot chicken, rotisserie style with rice. It was delicious. We ate with our hands, and sat and talked with the Afghani commanders, it was almost like a family dinner. This was our time to get to know them and for them to get to know us. After we finished our meal, they invited me to meet the elders. This was an important victory. It was like meeting your new girlfriend's parents; things were getting serious.

Somehow we got through the day, we had three meetings total. The commanders always received us well, but not always the villagers. On the dirt roads of the surrounding villages, they'd yell at us, and some would throw rocks as we were conducting foot patrols and when we passed by in our armored tactical vehicles.

Before we left the area, the unit we were replacing had to step aside and say their goodbyes. We stood outside, chatting with the men. They showed us the ropes, and told us what we needed to know about the roads, the terrain, and which routes to take in case someone got hit. It was important for us to know the landscape and the patterns of life in the area, so that if anything looked out of the ordinary we could identify threats right away.

One of the soldiers pointed out across the desert in the distance, a nearby route by Highway 7, which was notorious for IEDs. "This is where we got hit," he said.

"Be careful," they said.

We waved goodbye to the men just as the sun was setting, and went back to the base.

Praise God

The next time we left the wire, I was patrolling an area near an intersection, walking up and down the rows of grapes growing there in the rocky soil. Nearby was a big tan barrier filled with sand, which everyone called a HESCO fighting position. On our way in, the outgoing unit mentioned this was another area where they were hit by an IED, and we had to be careful every time we dismounted or were patrolling the area.

I was walking down a long row of grapes when I got a call on the radio. "Helicopter surveillance says someone has a suicide vest near the HESCO fighting position."

That was right next to us; all my senses were on alert.

The helicopters could see into the roofless Afghani structures from above, and had spotted something suspicious. They gave us a grid of where we needed to go, and said, "Go check it out and clear it."

Suicide vests were particularly dangerous because by the time you got close enough to the person wearing it to clear it, they could detonate. Even if you were fifty feet away, it was dangerous. I had to get the platoon there, and I had to go personally clear it. Choosing which men to take with me was an unpleasant chore. Some of them had families with kids. I decided to just bring the translator and our headquarters element, consisting of a forward observer (FO), and the radio operator. The problem was that I couldn't tell our translator that there was a suicide vest where we were going.

JOSEPH R. PEREZ JR

I told our linguist, "Hey, we need to check out this house, but keep your distance when we do it. We may have to ask them to come out with their hands up."

Slowly, we approached, and I noticed instead of a cut-out there was an actual door on the front of the house. I was trying to be as quiet as possible, but our linguist ran up and started knocking. I almost lost it and I yelled, "JC, STOP!"

He withdrew his hand from the door with a bewildered expression on his face.

Eventually, someone opened the door and there were people inside, but no suicide bomber. Thankfully, it was a false alarm, either that or they decided not to detonate it.

This was the first time I realized that the decisions I had to make, and the lives of my men—everything depended on my focus and preparation. This was everything I had trained for, and yet once you were in it, it was totally different.

Another night we were out on patrol, and we got instructed to do a handoff with another company within our same battalion. They were taking over our area for patrol because they had more people. The sky was pink on the western horizon, and I knew the outgoing team needed to get there while it was still light enough to do the introduction between the local leaders and the guys taking our place.

Just as I was introducing the local police commanders to the incoming platoon leaders, one of the guys from the platoon ran up and said, "We need you to listen to this on the radio."

"What's going on?" I asked.

"We need you to come right now," he said.

Over the radio I heard someone say, "We have a rotary wing aircraft, a helicopter, that's circling over a village and we can see someone carrying a rocket. We need you to go and get eyes on and investigate."

In the back of my mind, I thought, *these helicopters are killing me.*

I looked at the grid coordinates in shock; it was right across the street from us. Right at the base of NO DRUGS mountain.

I said, "Roger. WILCO." (Short for "will comply.")

My commander called me on the radio and said, "Make sure you bring the Afghan commanders with you, we want them to start doing clearances," reminding me one of our goals was a handover from the United States to the Afghan Army and Police Commanders so that they could defend themselves and operate independently.

I called the local Afghan police commanders and told them, "As promised, I will let you know anything I know, and they just told me there's someone with a rocket across the street."

I'll never forget this, he said, "Ok, but first we have to pray."

The timing couldn't have been worse, but I had to respect their religion. We agreed to go get eyes on the person, secure the area, and then the police commander and everyone from his compound would meet us there and clear the threat afterward.

Entering the coordinates into the GPS, we arrived shortly at the exact location where the person with the rocket was allegedly seen. Right before we stopped the truck, the helicopter pilot called on the radio and said, "We're out of fuel, we have to return to base now."

"Roger," I said. We were on our own.

We parked the vehicle and started looking around the area. The sun had set and now it was dark, which made it even more difficult to orient ourselves. It felt like all eyes were on me. It would be a split decision whether or not we'd have to engage the enemy. One of the squad leaders looked at me and said, "This is the part where I need you to tell me what you want me to do and where to go."

Knowing that every decision I made could cost us our lives, I told the first squad to take the east side of the building, the third squad would take the west side, and my guys would come from the north. The teams split up. As we approached the target building, I glanced down at my GPS and realized I was standing right at the grid coordinates where the rocket sighting was reported. A chill went down my spine. I was literally in the middle of a wide-open space, with houses all around me. We could have been hit from any direction.

One of the houses had a light on inside, and I gestured to my men, "Let's take this building."

Out of the corner of my eye, I saw movement. One of the squad leaders went up to the building and ran inside at full speed. All of us froze in the darkness, silent. We had weapons ready. This particular squad leader was tall with an athletic build, I could instantly tell it was him by his shadow and his gait. *Are you serious? What is he doing?* I thought.

Instantly, we put our weapons down, to avoid friendly fire. There was no rocket detected inside, just a family, but I was so angry at this squad leader for running inside. I felt like screaming at him, but instead, I let everyone know to secure the area until the Afghan police showed up. After the commanders had cleared all the buildings, I pulled the squad leader aside and said, "I want to speak with you after the patrol." I was furious.

We gathered everything up and went back to the base and debriefed. I needed time to cool down. Exhausted, I started typing up my after-patrol report on an old laptop. The sergeant let me know he was heading out and the squad leader I wanted to speak with would be in right after so we could talk. A few minutes later, the door to my office slowly crept open. Right at that moment, I heard the Spirit say to me, "How many times have I forgiven you?"

Suddenly, I wanted to break down and cry. *Every time*, I thought. *Every. Single. Time.*

My whole demeanor changed, and Bible verses began to run through my mind. I thought, *Christ died for my sins. Christ always forgives. Love thy neighbour as thyself.* Looking at the squad leader standing there, I had so many things I wanted to say to him, but now I didn't know what to say. I was overwhelmed.

I said, "If someone had walked out with a rocket ready to detonate it, there is no way I would have ordered the shot, because it might have hit you—what were you thinking?"

"It won't happen again," he said.

We hugged, but there was a tension between us. I sensed there was more to the story that he wasn't telling me. I never quite understood why he ran into that building. He was so professional and so good at his job, it was all so confusing. Despite my lack of understanding, all I knew was that God always forgave me, so I had to forgive him, and I left it at that.

Years later, when I'd gone back to Colorado Springs, I was assigned to teach a Sunday School lesson at my church. It was Thursday, and I still didn't have any lessons for church that Sunday. So, I prayed for God to give me one. Right after I did this, I got a text message at work that said, *"Is this Lieutenant Perez?"*

It was that same squad leader from years ago. He said he owed me an apology and then he proceeded to tell me a story that finally revealed to me the reason why he'd put his life in danger that day in Afghanistan.

He said, "When I was in EMT school the first time, before deployment, my wife had our first and only boy. He came a couple weeks premature, and wasn't in the best condition when he came to us. Well, a couple nights later the nurses in NICU told me that I needed to say my last goodbyes because he wasn't getting any better and it was looking like he was going to slip away in the next couple hours, or maybe days.

"That night I was in the worst mood ever, just blaming everyone for everything and getting mad at God for doing this to me and my family. Suddenly I just switched over and I ended up 'making a deal' with Him...and I know it's going to sound crazy but I told Him that I would gladly trade my life for my son's and God could take me during this deployment if he would just spare my son.

"The next day, my son was so much better, he was once and for all stable, he got the tube taken out of his stomach, and the day after that they told us we could take him home. So honestly, I thought God had accepted my offer. And that's why I would run into any building, volunteer to be the lead truck on every mission, or the point man. I volunteered for anything and everything, no matter how dangerous. In my mind, I was honoring my end of the deal.

"I feel horrible now that I have been out for a while with the way things went down. I didn't know how to deal with the fact that I wasn't going to see my family again and I took it out on a lot of people, but you got the most of it for some reason. Some nights I still can't sleep because I am still so grateful and surprised that I made it back. To be honest you are the only person I have shared this with because I needed you to know that I'm truly not a jerk, just dealing with some tough times and crazy circumstances. So, all in all, I am truly sorry for the way I treated you and blew up on you the first mission we went out on together."

Stunned, I told him it was okay. I understood. Here, I thought my situation was hard because of the tough position his actions had put me in, but I had no idea that he did what he did because he thought he wasn't going to come back and ever see his family again. He expected to give his life for his son.

Then, I asked him if it was okay to share his story as my Sunday School lesson as long as I kept out the names. He agreed. The lesson in Sunday School that day was titled, "Praise God."

Praise God that Jesus showed us to do the right thing and forgive others. Praise God every day. Praise God even when I don't understand (which can seem like always). Because if I hadn't trusted God, and listened to that still small voice, I never would have understood.

CHAPTER THREE
Angels before IEDs

We had just completed our mission, and we were on our way back, when the truck overheated.

It was a common occurrence, as we had to repair our military vehicles with whatever parts were available in Afghanistan, and they were often low quality. As we pulled over by the side of the road to let the engine cool off, I dismounted from the truck to have a look around. We were really close to the base, just north of it, maybe 150 feet from the gate of the compound. From where I was standing, I could still see the HESCO fighting position.

I radioed our headquarters to let them know we had stopped. I glanced around me, squinting into the distance, looking for anything out of place. We were in an open area, so we had to make it quick.

Some of the guys got out of the truck, and I said, "We need to maintain security, we only have five to ten minutes."

After the vehicle cooled down, we got in and drove back to base for some much needed rest. The Romanians would be taking over the patrol for us for the remainder of the evening.

In addition to the U.S. troops in Afghanistan, Romania had also sent men and women to support us as allies during Operation Enduring Freedom. They had their own compound, close to ours. Maintaining a twenty-four-hour presence outside the wire was next to impossible with just one platoon; we had to sleep at some point. So, the Romanians filled in for us that night, and helped cover the area, specifically the perimeter of the base. It was really helpful.

The very next day I woke up and heard the news. There had been an IED strike at the exact place where the truck had overheated and we'd dismounted. The Romanians had been hit.

The news shook me.

Trying to regain my focus, I asked about the details of the strike: What explosives were used? Was it a pressure plate? A remote control? Anything they could tell us might give us some clues as to what to look for next time. Suspicious wiring, a spotter, someone physically there to detonate the device. I wanted to make sure I could spot anything out of place to keep my men safe.

It was a remote controlled IED, which meant that somebody—the Taliban—had come within fifty meters of the wire. They'd built it at night and planted it, and they were that willing to get that close to our security to do it. In order to activate a remote controlled IED, they had to have someone watching the whole time, to know when to detonate it. It was very disturbing.

I asked if anybody had been hurt. After a pause, they said, "It was bad. Pretty bad."

"They're getting really close to our compound, be on the lookout," they said.

We briefed everybody, but in the back of my mind I was thinking, *this is crazy. It was right where we were yesterday.* It was almost like we were being watched, and the danger was getting closer and closer.

The next incident occurred right after this. After one of our patrols, we heard that some of the local villagers were rioting. We had just gotten back from our daytime patrol, so another platoon would be taking care of the mission.

Two minutes later, I got the call. The platoon on patrol had forgotten to bring their translator with them, could we go back out and handle it? I was so frustrated, all I wanted to do was eat dinner and go to sleep. We had just gotten back. *How do you forget your translator?*

I rounded up my men, and went back out, and we were immediately told there was a vehicle borne IED that needed to be cleared in the area. The CIA was there waiting to meet with us at the site, as well as the bomb squad (Explosive Ordnance Team), they'd even brought in bomb defusing robots.

One of the leaders from the bomb squad said, "We still need someone to physically clear it."

I thought, *isn't that what you guys are here for?*

Recalling my original intent and the request I'd made to God about bringing my men home safe, I wasn't willing to send in any of my guys. So, I had to do it myself.

I told the men, "Stay here."

It was pitch black, 9 P.M. maybe, and I could hardly see a foot in front of my face. Slowly, I walked up to the structure, it was just an open space with four walls, completely empty except for a white van conspicuously parked in the corner.

I took a few steps towards the van, anticipating an explosion with every second. Every nerve in my body was tingling and my muscles were taut, it was surreal. It reminded me of walking through the house without the lights on, when you can only see just enough to make out the vague shapes around you, but not well enough to feel certain of what you're stepping on.

The van was something resembling an old VW bus, but when I looked inside it was immaculate. It was almost too clean, like it had been prepped. I made a quick survey of the interior of the vehicle, there was nothing in there. "Hey, it's all good," I yelled.

I went back to the base in a state of shock. Even though there had been no IED, I couldn't shake the sinister feeling that van had given me. Later in deployment, we found out that the same van was used in an IED strike, on Highway 7, just outside the base.

One Day Off

We had just one day off, and that was it. Another platoon in the unit was out patrolling the area for us while my men and I relaxed as best we could in the heat.

I was stretched out on my bed, feet up, trying to take a much needed nap. I heard a buzzing sound, looked down, and saw I'd missed a call on my phone from an unknown number. I thought, *if it's important they'll call back.* When I woke up twenty minutes later, I saw I had missed six calls from that same number. I sat up in bed and said, "This is important."

The calls were from one of the Afghan police commanders we had met. He was speaking so rapidly in Pashto I could barely understand him. I had routinely been giving out my cell number to all the locals, so they could reach me. I always told them, "If you have info about the Taliban, call me."

I had been studying Pashto, but all I could think to say was, "My name is Perez."

He kept talking as if I understood him. I said, "I'm sorry, I don't know what you're saying." I called JC, our translator, and told him the situation. I said, "I think this is important. Someone keeps calling me, please call them and then call me back and let me know what the situation is."

Five minutes later, JC called back and said, "They found an IED."

Crap.

My first instinct was to warn the platoon on patrol covering for us. They were out there somewhere and if I didn't get this information to them, they might get hit.

I said, "JC, ask him where the IED is, get some type of identification."

Quickly, I threw on my PT's, the training uniforms we wore when we were off shift, and ran to the main command post, about a mile away. I couldn't call our leadership with sensitive information over a non-secure line. I remember pumping my arms and legs as hard and fast as I could, and then trying to control my breathing in case I received a call. In the HQ element, I stood there just waiting for the call. Under my breath I muttered, "Come on, JC, give me something."

The phone rang, it was JC. "I found out...they told me it's planted where you parked your trucks when you came to meet with the commanders for your patrol," he said.

It was an area that was very familiar to me. Just a few days ago, we had been working with that particular police commander and we had parked next to a grape row farm, near an opening alongside the walls that gave us access, so we could dismount and meet the police commander. I needed to relay this information to the unit on patrol. In my mind I was wondering, "What is going on? Every place we go, it seems like there's an IED..."

I told the command post, "Heads up, we just got an IED confirmation call. Here is exactly where it is."

The IED was planted on a road near Highway 7. We were warned not to use this road, but sometimes we had to since it was one of the only ways to reach certain areas and in particular, this police commander's unit. The unit on patrol might have to go there, so the HQ element called them on the radio and let them know on the map which area to avoid. Luckily, they found it, identified it, and got someone to defuse it. No one was hurt, this time.

"Stay Safe."

During my deployment, I constantly found myself having to choose between eating, sleeping, or working out. You could never get all three in one day, it was always too busy. There was a decent gym on base, but it was a twenty-minute walk across the motor pool, so to save myself some time, I started doing a "beach body" style program called Insanity. I actually cleared an area out behind the living quarters by the trash receptacles and swept away some of the debris, and worked out right next to the trash cans. It was convenient, and it worked for me.

Of course the guys gave me a hard time about it. Sometimes I was back there, and people would pass through to throw away trash. They'd laugh and snicker, "Is that your stay-at-home-mom workout?" I guess it was a popular workout for women, but I didn't care, I needed to stay in shape.

One day, I had some down time on my hands and I decided to go get a workout in. I brought my laptop down and said to our platoon sergeant, "I'm going to do Insanity."

"Ok, cool, I'm going to go lift real weights," he joked.

I went down to my little workout area and got down to business. Almost as soon as I finished my workout and started my cool down, another platoon leader came up and started talking with me.

He was only back there to throw away trash, but he stood there the whole time talking to me. I was exhausted and sweaty, but I didn't mind his company, it just felt really strange. I hadn't spoken to him much before, but now we were chatting like we'd been friends our whole lives.

We started talking about going home to Colorado after deployment, and maybe hanging out, skiing and snowboarding together. Normally, I never make plans with anyone, because I'm always scared I won't be able to keep my promise. Somehow, I found myself saying, "Yes, definitely, we'll go snowboarding."

It was so weird.

When my cool down was done, I said to him, "Hey, I'm done, I'll walk back with you."

We walked back through the living area together, chatting and joking around. When we reached the area where our paths parted ways—I was headed straight back to our platoon's living area and he had to turn left—he suddenly stopped. He said, "Hey man I'm going on patrol."

He was patrolling the area we had just finished patrolling. I just had this overwhelming feeling, standing there. I turned back to face the trash cans again, and I heard the Spirit clearly say, "Stay safe, stay safe—tell him to stay safe."

I had never felt anything like that.

I reached out my hand to him and said, "Stay safe."

The moment he shook my hand, I saw two tall translucent blue angels hovering over him. Tall as statues, majestic warriors, protectors. I couldn't understand what I was looking at, but I knew they were angels. I remember it felt like I was physically stunned, but specifically remember not being scared. There was something about them that felt harmless and yet so majestic and powerful. Taken aback, I was too shocked to say anything. He just turned and walked away, and I went back to our living area.

I didn't tell anyone. For some reason I had to go back up to the command post right afterwards, and when I walked in, everyone was huddled around the radio. It's like coming home to find ambulances outside your home. *Something happened*, I thought.

"What's going on, is everything ok?"

"We're waiting for a nine line medevac," someone said.

A nine line medevac is called over the radio only when a medical evacuation is necessary, usually after there has been an attack, or there were troops in contact, or someone had been hit by an IED, and they need immediate medical attention.

"What happened?" I asked.

"One of the units that just left the wire was hit by an IED."

That was the platoon leader's unit I just spoke with after working out. My heart sank. I didn't interrupt or talk to anyone, I simply said, "Do you have any info?"

"We know one was killed in action, and one is wounded—it's not looking too good."

I didn't ask which truck got hit, I almost didn't want to know, because I didn't want it to be that platoon leader. After this, I went into my office and shut the door and started praying, "God please bring them back safe."

Later they told me the lead truck had gotten hit, it was in the area we were responsible for. The platoon leader wasn't in that truck. Shortly after that, I learned it was in the same area we had patrolled right before the handoff. Then, I found out the driver who had been injured had died as well as the squad leader. Two men had died.

A few nights before this, I had been out by the trash area, and I saw the squad leader out there smoking a cigarette. I can't explain why it was significant to me, but this moment struck me, and I remembered it. As I walked back to the living quarters after hearing the news of his death, I was thinking about that moment. "I just saw him, too."

This was a difficult time. The only thing I could think was how could I help this platoon leader and his platoon? Our commander talked with us and told us their platoon won't be going out in sector again for the next few days. "We're going to do patrols and cover the area for them."

I called my dad for support, he grew up around Flint, Michigan near a lot of gang violence, he was also in the Army. He might have some insight. I asked him, "What do I say?"

Later, I went and bought a large American flag to give to the platoon leader on behalf of our platoon. One of the soldiers in our platoon was in The Old Guard who guarded the Tomb of the Unknown Soldier prior to being assigned to our unit. I asked him to fold the flag and let him know it would be for the platoon that was hit. It was the least I could do.

Every night after this I laid in bed and thought back to the vision I'd had of two angels standing over this platoon leader, guarding him, and I wondered about the significance of it all. I don't believe in coincidences; somehow I was receiving direct messages from the divine. The question was, the next time it happened, what should I do about it?

CHAPTER FOUR
Going Home

Just prior to leaving Afghanistan, we were assigned to be the alternate quick reaction force (response force on standby) on a mission that ended up going downhill fast.

This particular mission involved a lot of senior officials who would be meeting to support local medical needs. Some of us, myself included, wondered if it would be a good idea to have one centralized location for so many senior ranking officials. At the end of the day, they outranked us and made the calls, so we all did our assigned duties. We were just there to provide recommendations and execute orders.

During the mission that morning, we heard an explosion, but this was common. Sometimes explosive ordinance would have to detonate ammunition or do controlled detonation for unexploded ordnance (commonly called UXO). Shortly after, while we were in our living area cleaning our weapons, I got the notification that I needed to go to our command post.

I was told that the meeting with the senior officials had been hit by a vehicle borne IED.

The lieutenant for the primary quick reaction force stood right next to me as we were being briefed on the details. He was my friend and someone I had attended ranger school with, we were both assigned the same unit. We looked over the grid coordinates of the

IED and received our intel brief and assessment. They put us on standby, ready to deploy. As we were being briefed, I looked at the position of where the IED had been detonated on the map. It was right off of Highway 7 by a local market and hospital. The day before we had dismounted almost in that exact same spot, maybe twenty meters west of it. I felt a lump in my throat forming. I told the battle captain, "Sir, I don't know if this means anything, but I know exactly where that is, that was our dismount point the day before on a joint mission with the local Afghan Commandos."

He nodded.

I was told to stand by and they would get every functional vehicle to evacuate immediately; we would be ready to support if needed. Our platoon would have to go do battle damage assessment the following day and clear the hospital. It was risky because the Taliban had learned some of the ways we operated, and most likely they'd be expecting us to return to assess the damage done. Thus, we were told to expect an attack, that something might be waiting for you. They said, "Look for anything unusual."

The difficult part was that the hospital was right along the highway, none of us had been inside it, and it would be difficult to identify a suicide bomber in such a congested area. We weren't sure what "normal" would look like after this. Were there going to be patients inside? Would we be stopped or would there be an invasion of privacy that would cause disruptions to the civilian population?

Then, they told me, "Don't forget to inspect the annex." I thought, *you've got to be kidding me. There's an annex too?*

However, I replied, "Roger, sir." (That's really about all that you can say in most situations.)

The next morning, as we mapped out our dismount locations and discussed security, it seemed as though there wasn't a "best approach." We just had to be as fast and thorough as possible. Our plan was to dismount on foot off of the highway, have our vehicles provide mounted security, move inside the hospital, tactically clear it, complete battle damage assessment, and return to the vehicles as fast as possible. We had seven minutes to do this (that was the response time for a vehicle borne IED in the area). I wondered, *should we block the highway with wire? Do we create a blocking position around the building? How many people need to be inside? How do we position our gunners in the trucks to maintain 360 security?* All these thoughts ran through my head as I evaluated the best way to safely do this.

Finally, we embarked on our mission. It was just me, our Radio Transmission Operator (RTO), one individual assigned to help maintain security, and our translator to help provide direction in the hospital and communicate with anyone inside. The cars were moving fast, my heart was pounding as we approached. The first thing I noticed was an unusually large group of people next to the hospital. *Suicide bomber,* I thought. I said, "Just keep going and make it fast. Everyone needs to be on alert."

As I exited the truck I told the platoon sergeant, "Get all the vehicles turned around and prepare for exfil." If anything happened, I wanted the vehicles to be ready for immediate evacuation. Right after I said that, I put the hand mic down, and as the ball of my foot hit the ground I could see a vision of myself in the dust that was kicked up from my boot. I was somehow looking at myself as I dismounted the truck. In that moment I could see my mom hugging me on the day I said goodbye to her in Colorado. Time slowed down. I could see her with her eyes closed tightly, her arms around my neck. It was such a strong vision, as if I was actually back in Colorado. It was almost like I was saying goodbye again and was able to see my family one last time. I thought in my mind, *this is the day I'm going to die.* Strangely, I was okay with it.

After that moment, everything jumped from slow motion to fast forward and suddenly we seemed to be moving a million miles a second. I yelled to our translator, JC, "This is it! We need to go this way, I need you to guide me through and we have to get a picture of everything."

One of the guys on the ground pointed, "I think it's over here to the right, the one with the red cross." Yup, that was the right one. We redirected and sprinted inside the hospital. Blood everywhere. I just remember blood on the walls as we made our way through the hallways of the clinic, while JC guided us through the building. Finally, in the last room in the hospital, I heard our platoon sergeant's voice on the radio, "We need to leave, we need to leave." I realized the building was clear and we ran back outside. It was then I remembered the annex.

I said, "JC, ask one of the workers if there is an annex." He pointed across a large opening. "You've got to be kidding me," I thought. We ran across, cleared it, and sprinted back to the trucks. We all got back safely, nobody was hurt. They told us later that the large gathering was a funeral for everyone that lost their lives in the attack the day before.

Through the rest of deployment we had similar situations. I remember going to an Afghan compound and the next day we found out there was a sniper attack there. Every single area we went to something happened either right before or right after we left. Eventually things started to slow down but we still had to maintain a twenty-four-hour presence and I remember being tired a lot. I always felt like I had to be ready, be ready for the unexpected.

During our patrols, we would typically be out for twelve to eighteen hours at a time. It gave me a lot of time to think. The more I thought, the more I started to look at the situation. I didn't write home very often because honestly there wasn't a whole lot of time, but while I was out on patrol I thought about my family and how we were growing closer in my absence. They started going to church and said they were praying for me, those were things that hadn't been said in a long time. It occurred to me that maybe if I didn't come home, my family's situation would improve. *God's going to use me to bring them closer together.*

With that, I started wondering about God's plan for my life. *Maybe this is it*, I thought. Maybe it wasn't God's will for me to come home. I had to accept this.

A passage from the Bible came to mind, when Jesus prayed before being crucified. In Luke 22 it says: "And he was withdrawn from them about a stone's cast, and keeled down, and prayed, Saying, Father, if thou be willing, remove this cup from me: nevertheless not my will, but thine, be done. And there appeared an angel unto him from heaven, strengthening him. And being in agony he prayed more earnestly: and his sweat was as it were great drops of blood falling down to the ground."

"Not my will, but thine, be done," these words kept going through my mind. I thought maybe all these instances were to keep me ready, just to be ready for what was coming. Who was I to think that I shouldn't be submitted wholly to God's will? Suddenly, I wanted to accept it, and know that God had a plan for me. From this moment forward, I started to think differently. I started to pray more, and I started asking for God's will in my life. I stopped caring what people thought, and started caring about what God thought, and what God wanted. How could I serve God better? I had a million questions for Him, and I knew He had all the answers. I felt like I could ask Him anything.

At the time, I remember thinking, "If I do make it home, I'm going to be different." Nevertheless not my will, but thine, be done.

Towards October, it had been roughly nine months into deployment, and people started getting antsy. They started asking things like, "When is the new unit getting in?" "What's going on?" "Do we have any dates?"

At the end of deployment there's so much going on; you're trying to coordinate with your family and get into the mindset of reentering civilian life. At the same time, you still have a job to do. Just weeks away from going back to the States, we got a mission—and it would require the most planning and coordination yet.

We were assigned an air assault mission—insertion by helicopter—and I was the one who was supposed to be leading it. They told us we needed to do a mission just outside of the base, there were some high value targets, and they needed us to hit these locations. These targets were associated with the Taliban. I had zero experience with helicopters, and a lot of planning needed to happen. My commander took lead on planning with the pilots. I began working with the platoon sergeant and squad leaders. They had all done this, and I wanted every ounce of input possible and to provide as much time training as they knew we would need. It was overwhelming to plan and prepare, but I trusted them.

This was the hardest mission we'd received since we'd gotten there. It was the most intelligence based, and it would be the first time we'd be dealing with the Taliban at the exact residences they were staying at. Some questioned why we were doing this so late in deployment, why not earlier. At the same time, we thought, *that's why we're here.* We needed to do it, because it was assigned to us and that's why we came.

The mission was this: we had to surround and isolate the living area where the targets were, go inside, and clear it. If people were there we had to take them and capture them, but we had to let the Afghan Uniformed Police take lead and do it. We were not supposed to go inside residences, so they had to do that. We had to be quick, and it would be at night. You couldn't do this type of mission during the day because there were civilians everywhere. The worst friction point was on the ground at night; there were so many unanswered questions— how would we link up with Afghan Uniform Police at night without compromising communication and location? They didn't have the radios or technology we had, and this posed a major problem. The big picture goal was to train and hand the mission over to Afghan forces, so they could operate autonomously. We had to support them, ultimately let them execute the site exploitation and deal with anyone inside, but we would still lead the operation. Thinking through all that was pretty difficult.

I had an idea. We had a military issue type of glow stick, called a chem light, but instead of phosphorescent it's infrared; once you crack them you couldn't see the "glow" unless you had a night vision device. I took some 550 cord and made necklaces with a chem light attached to the end and went to meet the police compound. I brought one to the Afghan police commander and said, "Hey, we're doing a mission together soon."

The commander looked at the "necklace" and frowned. He expressed that he didn't think this would work.

I took a glow stick and cracked it. I said, "When we meet, I need you to crack this and wear it. No one will be able to see you but us." I wanted to crack the chemical light in front of him so he could visually see that you could not see anything with the naked eye when the chemical light was being used. He agreed.

He wanted to know when the mission would be. I said, "I can't tell you when it is, but it's going to be in the middle of the night."

I tried to ease their fears by telling them that nobody would see them, but us. They were hesitant, though, and I left the meeting with no idea whether they were going to listen to me, or work with us on this. At the end of the day, I did everything I could. I had to rely on their word.

When we left, I said to the guys, "I hope they don't mess around with the glow sticks and break it before they need it." They only last twenty-four hours, so if they cracked it early we wouldn't be able to positively identify them except for in person, which could pose a threat at night if you can only do so from a short distance.

After this it was rehearsals, practicing getting on and off the aircraft, sitting in the order we'd be inside the helicopter. It was hot and dark, and the gear was cumbersome; everyone was sick of it. We just wanted to get the mission done.

I met with the pilots and they explained how we'd strategically conduct the mission with an effort of not having anyone notice us. They told me what we had to look out for, even livestock, or roaming animals that might hamper a safe nighttime landing. We created backup plans and contingency after contingency. My mind was exhausted.

At that point all of us were thinking, *let's just do this thing.*

Finally, the night came. Everyone was in order, and we knew what we had to do. Everybody was a little nervous because you never knew what was going to happen. The helicopter could malfunction, we could get shot at, anything can really happen. Once we got in the aircraft, all I remember is that you couldn't hear anything. You really had to project your voice to ensure everyone heard it. The look on everyone's faces said everything. We were all excited to go home, but first we had to do what we had to do.

We actually landed in what felt like swamp land. When I exited the helicopter my boots sank into the ground; I was standing in something soft and saturated. *Please let this be mud,* I thought. It reminded me of a swamp during ranger school, it was hard to walk in. We were in a tactical formation, but it was disorienting, pitch black.

At that moment, I got a call on the radio—it was one of the squad leaders. He told me the point man had dropped the GPS and it broke. We couldn't use it. I acknowledged his response and we kept moving. I thought, *so that's how this mission is going to start?*

Thankfully, we all had a GPS on our wrists, so it was ok. But it felt like it wasn't the best start. We walked across the field, in the deep mud, out in the open. I could see the village in the distance. I immediately called the Afghani police to let them know we'd just landed; they needed enough time to come meet us. We'd chosen a local landmark as our appointed meeting place.

I said, "Crack the necklaces" and my translator JC translated it to the police.

Above us were unmanned aerial vehicles (a fancy word for a drone), watching us, as well as the whole city. I got a call from my squad leader, he said, "It looks like a group of military aged males are in a tactical formation...it looks like they have AK47's, and they're headed towards us."

Ok, *the Taliban already knew we were coming.* That was my immediate thought. Or these guys were working with the Taliban. Or something else happened. There should be no reason why there was a group of men moving towards us with AK47's. I told our squad leader to be ready in case we made contact.

He said, "Wait. Don't overreact."

We were prepared to fire our weapons when we realized the "armed men" were the Afghan Uniformed Police. I thought back to some advice I had been given before going active duty, *trust your NCOs.*

It was such a relief, but it was a close call. We met with them and conversed briefly. They even brought the necklaces. Together, we moved slowly through the mud. At one point, we were moving too slowly and our commanding officer began to get upset. *Hurry up. If you don't get us there on time, you will no longer be a platoon leader.* We were behind schedule. I knew we needed to get there on time, but safely. I always remembered how information was passed down, and I couldn't control how others treated me, just how I treated others. I told my commanding officer, "Roger, sir." I went to our lead squad leader and said, "Don't worry about the timeline, just get us there." I had no idea if that would work.

We arrived muddy and on foot, at our destination, on time. It looked like the Taliban had gotten a heads up because nobody was there that we had expected when we arrived. the Afghan Police began clearing the sites and we finished our mission. I didn't know what to make of it. We hit all the targets, and took pictures of people inside, but they weren't the ones we were looking for. Slowly we trudged back in the mud. Once we got into the helicopter, a weight was lifted off of me. Once we were finished, you could feel the relief. We landed at the base, everyone was safe, and once again we could focus on just going home. Now we were in transition mode, packing our gear.

Right around this time, near the end of my deployment, I had another strange experience. One night I was walking back from the command post with a few other men, it was probably 9 or 10 P.M. It was pitch black enough to see the stars, but you could still see shapes of things around you. In the distance, a few feet ahead of us, I saw a commander. This wasn't unusual, I figured he was going on a night patrol. For some reason, I recall this moment specifically—he was climbing up into a truck, standing on the steps, and I saw a bright shining spotlight on him. It's hard to explain, it wasn't a spotlight from the sky, like a beam, it was just shining above him and on him. A bright, yellowish orange light like a fire lit the sky. I thought, *what is that?*

At that moment, I remember I had this strong feeling something was going to happen, but I wasn't sure what. He was wearing an anti-remote control IED device, I could see the antenna sticking out from where I was standing. I remember watching him climb into the truck with this celestial light beaming on him. I didn't know what was happening.

I kept walking in silence and kept it to myself. The next morning, I woke up and found out that the commander had gotten hit by a vehicle borne IED.

That night his unit was out doing a patrol in the area, near the highway. They noticed a van that kept driving suspiciously around them; it looked out of place. As soon as the van got close enough, they detonated it. I was shocked when I found out that it was the same "suspiciously clean" one I had cleared earlier. They'd loaded it full of explosives, and when the military truck went by, it got detonated.

Some people broke their legs, some got injured. The commander I saw was unscathed, but everyone around him got hurt. I hardly had time to process this information, when you're on deployment, everything is so fast paced. You're just reacting and doing everything you can to help and support. One thing that seemed to be a repeating theme was that all this was happening really close to where we were, and it seemed to be getting closer every time. It turned out my observation wasn't just a hunch, the danger was very real. I returned from deployment November 2014, just about nine months in. The day we went back home, and the last plane took off on our departure day, a series of rockets hit the place we were living. I heard the news when I was back in the United States. We were the last patrol out of that area of Afghanistan.

CHAPTER FIVE
This Could Be Your Last Night

Just before we left Afghanistan, we were told we'd be leaving again in a year.

It was very bittersweet for us. We were all so excited to go home and do normal American things like eat Chipotle, drive our cars, and just be able to enjoy a weekend. After they told us that, it felt like there was no end in sight. The second I got home I enjoyed time off but mentally started preparing to deploy again.

Prior to our deployment, I was selected with a few other people to work for our senior commander. Shortly after we began working, we found out we would actually be staying in the United States through the deployment. I had just a little bit of time to settle into the new house I'd bought when they told me there was a new position opening up in Baumholder, Germany for Battle Captain.

It was one of those jobs where you'd be working long hours for the same pay, which is why when they announced it nobody jumped at it, because everybody knew it would probably be a drudge job working in an office.

After thinking about it and talking to one of my close friends, I decided to volunteer for it. When I said I'd take the job, one of the field grade officers shook my hand and said, "You just bought yourself a ticket to Germany!"

I went into this knowing it would be difficult, but I felt like the job would be a good learning opportunity. I knew I'd probably get yelled at a lot, but I would also get exposure to higher level thinking and I'd grow and learn a lot.

Once I got there, it was exactly as I'd imagined; long days, and very little time to learn. I was working for a one star General, a Lieutenant Colonel, and a Major. It was extremely fast paced. This was the first time an armored unit had been deployed to Europe. As Battle Captain, I was responsible with the staff for tracking movements and there were nonstop updates and meetings to coordinate with units in different countries like Italy, Poland, and Germany.

I was overwhelmed fast, and my only saving grace was the weekends.

Every weekend I would try to go somewhere new and decompress. One weekend I went to Milan, Italy to visit a friend (coincidentally named Milan). After spending time with my friend and their family, I felt relaxed and ready to return to Germany. Little did I know this evening would lead to something awful.

My flight was later that day, so I took the bus to the city center, and luckily I remembered right where the shuttle had dropped me off that morning. As I was walking to that spot something told me that was where I needed to go. After about a minute, a bus pulled up that said Airport on it, but I had seen other buses with the same destination on it, and I had a funny feeling about it. Regardless, I didn't want to miss my bus, so I got on and showed the driver my ticket and I asked if he was going to the airport. He replied, "Yes!"

"It'll be fast, I can take the speed lanes, a taxi will be more expensive," he said.

I had a weird feeling in my stomach, but I was pushing the schedule and I was late. So, I sat down in my seat thinking, *ok, I'm going to the airport.*

Once we got to the airport, I immediately went to the airline counter where the attendant looked at my ticket and said, "What are you doing here?"

I didn't know there were three airports in Milan, and apparently, I was in the wrong one. The idea occurred to me that maybe I could take a taxi to the other airport, so I asked, "How long will it take?"

"By the time you get there your plane will have left," she said.

My only option was to buy an entirely new ticket from that airport for a flight leaving in a few hours. This worried me because in the military you had to give notice of leave, it was like putting in vacation time at a job. And if I wasn't back Friday morning, I would be considered AWOL. The last thing I wanted to do was call my boss and tell him I went to the wrong airport and needed to extend my leave.

So, I bought the ticket and thought, *well, I'll get there a little later than planned and I'll just drive back. I don't need much sleep.*

The attendant was really sympathetic. She handed me the plane ticket and said, "We'll get you back tonight."

When I landed, I was so tired. The first thing I did was get a coffee. It was a two-hour drive from the airport, and I would have just enough time to get home, brush my teeth, shower and go to bed. But at least I wouldn't be AWOL.

I got on the Autobahn where cars regularly drive 100 miles per hour or more, but making sure I stayed in the slow lane. The roads were cold and dark and while I was driving my windows started to fog up on the inside. I tried to wipe the condensation off with my hands, but I still couldn't see a thing and it was concerning as I was driving at night.

The car was different from the Italian rental car I was used to driving earlier that week, so I couldn't find the switch to turn up the heat to clear the windows. I took my eyes off the road for one second to find the knob to defog the windows, found the switch, and the next thing I saw was a set of headlights right in front of me. I hit the brakes as hard as I could and immediately I felt the impact on my chest. My car slammed into the vehicle in front of me and swerved off to the left. To this day I don't remember seeing any cars in front of me the entire time up until impact.

I remember being in a daze. It was like getting hit hard in the stomach. Every breath I took I inhaled smoke, it felt like I was choking for air. The car was still moving, so I tried to brake, but I had lost all control of the brakes and acceleration.

I was desperately trying to think. The steering still worked, so the only thing I could think of was to ram my car into the railing, because at least I'd be on the shoulder and my car wouldn't be on the Autobahn where it could get hit. I took the steering wheel and turned it as fast as I could until I could feel the rail skidding against the side of the car and it came to a complete stop.

The passenger side door was stuck, it was flush with the railing. At that moment everything was happening so fast. My window was rolled down so I ended climbing out the window of the driver's seat. Once I got out of the car, shaken and bruised, I realized the song that had been playing while all this happened was "How Great Thou Art" by Carrie Underwood.

In Germany there was a law that if you passed a motor crash you had to assist. After a few minutes, someone pulled up and asked if I was ok, and if anyone was behind me. I said, "Yes, I hit him."

It was so dark, I had no idea who I had hit.

The weight of what I had done came down on me, I felt so terrible. *What if I caused a fatal injury? What if there was a kid in the back seat?* I had no idea what was happening. The motorist reversed to check on the other driver and called the Polizei. When the police arrived, they said there was a wife, husband, and kid in the other car. My stomach dropped, but thankfully, they were ok.

They sent me to the hospital. I immediately texted my boss from my cell phone and told him about the incident. Thankfully he wasn't upset. He just told me, "You may want to try to get transferred to an American Military Hospital as well so they can take a look and get everything documented."

I replied, "Ok, sir."

Every time I asked the doctor to transfer me, they told me no. I had to get a CAT scan and they told me by German law I would have to stay overnight. I remember the nurse telling me that night, "You may have internal bleeding and may not wake up in the morning," and then they just left.

I prayed about it. As I rested my head and closed my eyes, I thought, *what if this is my last night? God has a plan. Nevertheless, not my will, but thine be done.*

The nurse's comments about not waking up in the morning made me so much more thankful when I did wake up the next day. I rolled out of bed feeling relieved, and went straight to the church in the hospital to pray. I sang "How Great Thou Art" out loud by myself in the hospital church. It didn't matter to me, but it felt like a one-on-one conversation and giving thanks to God. Sitting in the church pew shedding tears of joy, I realized how everyday truly was a gift, whether we realized or not.

I kept feeling the need to get transferred to another hospital. It didn't have to do with the quality of care of where I was, but just a general feeling that I just needed to be transferred. I kept asking the hospital staff, and again and again I was told no. Finally, I prayed about it, saying, "Not my will, but thine be done, God." Then, I walked downstairs to the cafeteria to get some food.

After looking at the food selection, I went to take some money out of my account, but the ATM kept denying my card. The cafeteria only took cash, so eventually I gave up and just walked outside to get some fresh air.

The second I walked back inside a woman I have never seen approached me and said, "Are you Joseph Perez?"

I said, "Yes."

She said, "My name is Bonnie De Jesus and I'm here to get you transferred to a military hospital."

I had never seen this woman before but I asked her, "Do you know what 'De Jesus' means?"

She told me no, and I told her it meant "from Jesus." I had just prayed about this, and after one phone call that she made I was told to get ready to be transferred to another hospital. It was too perfect to be a coincidence!

As they were loading me into the van, I remember Bonnie said, "I'm glad I could be someone's angel today."

Once I was transferred to my room in the military hospital, they examined me and told me I had no life-threatening injuries. While I was waiting to be discharged, I got my Bible out and began to read. The assistant nurse assigned to me was a Christian. She noticed me reading the Bible and asked what I was reading. I told her, "Just reading some Bible verses."

We started talking about our faith and specifically, the spiritual realm. She admitted she had recently watched a horror movie about demons and it was bothering her. She said she was never someone to look over her shoulder in the shower but she felt like something was watching her.

I told her that when you watched movies about demons it could be a way to allow demons to enter into your life. I told her that if it happened again, to command the demon to leave and to play music about the blood of Jesus.

As we continued talking, I could see some type of malevolent spirit at the door of the room. It looked translucent.

We went on talking for a while, but I could see the spirit in the corner of my eye, just hovering there by the door. Then the spirit came inside and went to the corner of the room. Finally, she noticed me staring at the corner, I looked back at her and I said, "I'm not trying to scare you, but I can see something in this room."

She replied, "I know, I can see you looking at it."

I played a song on my phone called *Nothing but the Blood* and demanded the demon to leave. I explained to her that being attacked was not always bad. If you thought about it like a sports analogy, you wouldn't double team the worst player on the opposing team, you'd double team the best player.

The spirit left the room, and she said she felt relieved.

I was anxious to get out of the hospital, so I asked if she could check on the status of my release. A few hours later, I was told I could go home.

A friend from work picked me up from the hospital. When he saw me he jokingly asked, "How's it going, Nascar?" He had a big grin on his face. He was referring to the accident of course. It had been one of the longest nights of my life and I was exhausted.

I just laughed and said, "Take me home."

Chapter Six
Angels Landing

"Who maketh his angels spirits; his ministers a flaming fire."

Once I returned from deployment I immediately began preparing to transition out of my platoon leader role, which was the introductory role that lasted about nine months and was the catalyst for your entire military career. For me it was a mixture of feelings, because your platoon leader role was the epitome of what you looked forward to in college, it's all you think about, so much emphasis is put on preparing you for it that you never think past it. Now that it was over, I thought, *what do I do now?*

They sent me up to work in our staff office, and everybody has to do it, but I really didn't want that role. Especially not after coming back from infantry and shooting real bullets, the last thing I wanted to do was sit in front of a computer all day.

I kept asking them, "Is there anything else I can do? Is there another role open?"

Eventually, I accepted my fate as a staffer. Even though I knew nothing about office work, I helped the new person transition in, we exchanged phone numbers, and I started learning my staff role in earnest. The entire time I hated it; I felt micromanaged, and my quality of life went down that year. Working forty- to sixty-hour weeks took its toll on me, I felt like I had very little personal free time. Every day I would come into the office and think, "Why am I here?"

I reasoned if all my time was spent working during the week, on the weekends I needed to travel. The problem was, one weekend a month I still had to do a twenty-hour shift for a staff duty position. It was frustrating. I started to think about traveling more and more, I planned little trips. Utah wasn't that far away from Colorado, and I'd always wanted to go to Moab. One day I saw the flights were only $100, so I thought I might as well go.

April 28th, 2017, I found myself on a trip to Utah. I didn't even bother booking a hotel, so I had no idea where I was going to stay that night, I would figure it out on the plane. I ended up flying into Las Vegas because it was quicker and cheaper (I think I spent less than $200 on the whole trip). After I landed, I got a rental car and just started driving across the desert to Zion National Park.

The drive to Zion bolstered me. I saw the endless skies out of the window of the car and thought about things. Even though it was four years after my deployment, I still hadn't fully processed what happened. I didn't want to face the emotions, so I rarely talked about it.

I had been listening to Christian and faith-based music that talked about God's grace and healing, and it put me into a grateful mindset. I found myself wondering, "What if things had turned out differently?"

I had always been thankful for my friends, family, and food on the table, but now I was grateful just to have all my limbs and the freedom to vote. One of the biggest realizations that struck me was that you were just as safe in an office behind a computer as you were behind a rock in Afghanistan. Wherever you go, God will be with you. It doesn't matter if you're in your suburban neighborhood or on deployment.

Turns out, my sister and her boyfriend were going to be in Zion around the same time, so we decided to meet up. The next morning, I decided to go for a quick run at the park, so I got on the first trailhead I could find and just started running. It was therapeutic for me, and I enjoyed running a lot.

My sister and her boyfriend took a different trail, but I kept an eye on the time so I could meet up with them where the trails intersected. After about a half hour I was running along, listening to music, and I ended up right behind them. There was a famous viewpoint in Zion National Park called Angel's Landing and I suggested we go check it out. We were tight on time and it was a long hike, it would be dark by the time we got back, but we decided to hike there anyway.

I remember my knee was giving me trouble, I had a brace on and I tightened it a bit. We started walking and it was the most gorgeous view, a deep valley with red rock and tan mountains. We were standing on a sheer cliff, and I don't know why it seemed like a good idea at the time, but I decided to do a handstand. Looking at this incredible majestic view, I was a little nervous about falling. Suddenly I had that feeling like when you look down and realize how high up you are, and I felt respect for the height. We took some pictures and then I slowly got down from the rock and started walking down.

On the way down, I glanced over at the valley. The sun was shining on the open grass and I wasn't sure what I was looking at, but I saw what looked like translucent figures in the distance. When I saw them, it reminded me of Afghanistan, but instead of seeing the figures hovering like they did over my friend in Afghanistan, they were fighting.

The whole time I was thinking, "Angels Landing. Why did they call it that?"

I remembered reading in the Bible about angels and demons fighting in a particular passage in Job, "Satan was in his presence and he felt the hairs on the back of his neck stand up."

The hair on my left arm was standing straight up. In that moment I wasn't scared, I knew I was looking at something special. I said to my sister, "Do you guys see that?" They were too far up the trail and they didn't hear me, they kept walking.

Suddenly, it felt like someone was standing next to me, my entire body felt a presence. When I looked back at the valley, the angels were still fighting. I remember thinking this was very real. I wasn't hallucinating, I was seeing something in a spiritual realm.

We ended up leaving Zion National Park after a few hours, we hiked around that day and when I left, what I had seen wasn't a surprise to me. I knew God was real. I never once thought, "Why am I seeing this?" I knew God wanted me to see it for a reason.

It made me think of the things I struggled with, like temptation. I had seen a fight between good and evil. After this, I often felt a presence or something in the room with me right before I went to sleep. When I was scared, I would recite the gospel to calm myself.

Cherubim

"Angels came and ministered unto him."

Shortly after my visit to Zion National Park, I started taking ball room dance lessons. I had just attended a friend's wedding and watched the dance rehearsal before the ceremony. They were waltzing around and I thought, *that looks really cool, I would love to do that.*

So I called around to some dance instructors in Colorado Springs and told them I wanted to learn how to waltz. I started taking lessons and I was surprised I got really into it. I didn't even have proper dancing shoes, but the instructors convinced me to compete in the ballroom dancing competitions. While I was at these big events, I got invited to take a group lesson and learn tango, salsa, and bachata. I absolutely loved it, so I switched from ballroom dancing to salsa.

I remember it was fun, but way harder than I thought it would be. The first thing my instructor told me was that if anything goes wrong, it's the guy's fault (the guys lead every move). My instructor and I started competing together and we took first place at a few events.

One day, I remember I was at the studio and we were getting ready for a competition, rehearsing some of our routine. The owner's wife was sitting on the floor and her newborn was crawling around. I noticed she was wearing the same colors as me, black pants and a blue top. I was just about to say, "Hey! we're matching!" when I saw two baby angels—cherubim—hovering over her, comforting her.

I was on the dance floor and I just stopped. It was strange because I'd never seen angels in a room like that, and I'd never seen baby angels either. Somehow I knew they were comforting her, like when you put your hand on someone and console them. I didn't say anything because I was in shock. I just kept looking at the figures, and I saw the same translucent blue light I saw in Afghanistan.

I said to my instructor, "I need a quick break."

When I came back, we started dancing again and I finished the routine, but I didn't tell anyone what I had seen. That night, I was texting my instructor and I sent her a bible verse that said, "Tomorrow is not promised."

She said, "Interesting you should say that, we just found out the owner's wife's family member was in an accident tonight on a river and was tragically killed."

I asked her, "When did that happen?"

"It just happened tonight," she replied.

It wasn't a coincidence that those two events happened like that, the angels were clearly comforting and consoling her. This experience opened my eyes. Every incident showed me how much protection there really was; the IED's; the angels fighting the demons; the baby angels comforting this woman even though she didn't even know what had happened to her brother yet. I knew that even if we don't see God taking care of us, He's still watching over us.

CHAPTER SEVEN
Has Anyone Here Seen Angels Before?

In 2017, when I was still active-duty military, I got sent to Oklahoma for the Captain's Career Course, Triple C for short. This was a mid-management level course for officers held at Fort Sill just outside of Lawton, Oklahoma. I was first Infantry, but I was switched to Air Defense as a Captain. I'd never spent a day in Air Defense, I knew nothing about it, so I saw this course as a positive way to learn about missiles.

Immediately when I got there I started looking for a church to get involved with. I was still in my U-Haul truck, everything was in boxes, I pulled into a church I had researched online. I pulled in and told the preacher, "I just arrived here and I'm interested in going to your church." I wanted to see what he believed doctrinally, to make sure we aligned. After a week or two, I felt this was where God wanted me to go.

I was also pursuing my MBA at the time in addition to the Captain's Career Course. So, if I wasn't in classes learning about missile defense tactics, I was at Starbucks studying for my MBA and trying to pass those classes. I felt really overwhelmed, and church was the only place where I felt like I could relax and decompress.

One day I was sitting in the back of church, tired. The pastor was telling a story about his mother who had passed away recently. He said when his mom was on her deathbed she asked everyone in the room with her, "Can you see them?" They looked around the hospital room, but they didn't see anything. "What are you talking about, it's just us."

"They're here!" She said, "You can't see them yet because it's not your time."

Then he said something that caught my attention and made me snap awake. He said, "Has anyone in this room ever seen an angel?"

It wasn't until this moment that I realized I hadn't processed all that had happened to me in Afghanistan. I hadn't really thought about it, but for the first time I was thinking maybe someone had experienced something similar to me. I hadn't told anybody yet, but I thought, *maybe I should share my story?*

Slightly, I raised my hand, but only far up enough so I could see it.

His sermon had a powerful effect on me, I was shaking nervously. Suddenly, I wondered, *why did I see an angel?*

Around this time I had met an elder Native American man in the church, Brother Bruce, who had begun mentoring me. After the sermon, I saw my mentor talking with the pastor. I walked up my mentor was standing close enough so he could hear the conversation and I said, "Is it okay if I tell you something?"

He said, "Yeah, sure."

"You know when you asked if anyone has seen angels in your sermon? I have."

I proceeded to tell him about seeing the two angels over James prior to his platoon getting hit by an IED. I said, "I don't know what this means, but I could see them."

Just the fact that I shared it was a relief. I could finally tell someone. Because he had shared a similar testimony in the sermon, that made it so much more real.

South Korea

After Lawton, I graduated with an MBA and in the same week I finished the Captain's Career Course. A huge weight was lifted off my shoulders. The only problem was I was going to start a new career in missile defense as a captain, and I still had no first-hand experience. I only knew what I had learned in textbooks. I found out right after this that they were sending me to South Korea, it would be the same year as the North Korean peace talks.

My first day in Korea, Kim Jong Un shot a missile over Japan. That was my very first day. The commander arrived and said, "Why am I finding out Kim is shooting missiles over us from CNN and not you?"

I was like, *this is not good.*

He was right, I was supposed to be the battle captain, but I had just gotten there hours ago. I decided to keep my head down and learn as much as I could, and I knew it was going to be a steep learning curve.

One of my outlets has always been fitness, but I disliked the PT program in Korea. Even though we attended PT every day there was never a workout plan, the gym was small and overcrowded, and most of the time we always ended up going for a run. There were a few trainers near where I lived and I got close with one of them, a girl named Kelly. She was an Air Force Academy grad, extremely fit, also I found out she was a Christian.

She was the trainer for the morning class, so I started working out with her. One day we were in the cross fit gym, we'd just finished an extremely hard work out and I was literally laying on the floor. We were talking about Christian music or Bible study and I'm not sure what prompted me to talk to her, but I said, "Can I tell you something I've never really told anyone before?"

I told her the story about James. When I was done talking, she looked stunned like she almost couldn't believe it. She was obviously taken aback, but I felt comfortable enough to tell her another story, the one about the angels in the dance studio. She was a writing major, and she told me I should write the story and share it with others. I wasn't a writer, besides the occasional research paper. But her encouragement and advice stayed in the back of my mind for a while.

I stayed in Korea for one year. This was an especially difficult year for me. One thing I always felt was that I got a lot of unwanted attention because I'd gone to Ranger school and had a tactical combat arms background. In the Infantry you carried heavy weight and shot machine guns—in missile defense they don't do that. The younger soldiers were interested in my stories and background, and they asked lots of questions about awards I'd received. I'd never really thought about it being something out of the ordinary, to me, it seemed normal. Everyone around me did the same thing, so it was expected. You'd wake up and they'd say, "Today we're going for a twelve-mile march or a five mile run, so let's get out there." It was just what you did in the Infantry.

Eventually the differences in our backgrounds developed into a jealousy among my peers. I tried to shrug it off, but it became frustrating. People told me if I wanted to stay in this branch and be successful, it would be "easy" because of my background. I didn't like that kind of work atmosphere or career path where I wouldn't be challenged. I didn't want to just coast through, I liked doing something that feels almost impossible. When I heard that, it felt a little cutthroat.

I started thinking about how much I wanted to get out of the military, multiple times per day. I wanted to stay and serve, but at some point, I thought *if this is what I think about so much, then I should probably move on.*

God put it on my heart to go back to school. After finishing the MBA, I was excited, but I had this feeling that I needed to go back. Like in the Bible when God told Moses to go, and Noah to go, just like them, at first I had my doubts, but it was clear He wanted me to pursue my doctorate. While I was in South Korea, I decided to apply to Liberty University, a faith-based school in Lynchburg, Virginia. A few weeks later I got the acceptance letter, I was in shock. I thought, *I'm not smart enough!*

The doctorate program was in business, specifically nonprofit management and leadership. It wasn't too expensive, only $40,000 total, but I'd be just getting out of the military and I wasn't sure if I'd have a job right away. Getting accepted threw me off. At first I didn't tell anybody, I was thinking *how do I do this?* I didn't want to go into debt, but I decided if I had to sell everything I owned and live out of my car that's what I'm going to do. If this was what God wanted me to do, I'm going forward.

One day I was talking to my boss, a female major in the Army. I told her I was thinking about going back to school and getting out of the military. To my surprise, she said, "You just have to make a decision, doesn't matter what it is, just do what's best for you."

It was the first time anyone in the military had told me to do what's best for my life, everyone else was about retention numbers and making the unit look good. That was a defining moment for me; I was going to get out of the military.

After this, I stopped thinking about how much I hated the job.

That's how I left Korea. I went in nervous, and I left transitioning into the civilian world, focusing on a doctorate degree. This would be a huge step for me as the military was all that I had known since college.

Tell James

The graduate program started in January 2019. I got back from Korea in November of 2018, right on Veterans Day.

My next big obstacle presented itself almost immediately. In the military when you spend time overseas you have what's called dwell time. For example, I had spent twelve months in South Korea, so I had twelve months guaranteed they would not deploy me. It was perfect. I had twelve months in the States, guaranteed, so I could prepare for my studies. Right away, I went to go introduce myself to my commander, and the first thing they told me was, "You're deploying to the middle east in two weeks."

They asked me to waive my dwell time. I hadn't even been in the U.S. for four weeks and that's what they told me. It hit me like a brick, I felt like a wall had collapsed on me.

Nobody wants to be a deployment dodger. People would pretend to get hurt on purpose so they wouldn't have to deploy. The way I saw it, you signed up to defend the nation, so don't turn around suddenly and say you can't do it. This is what we signed up for. But the other side of me thought, *there is no way I can be deployed and focus on my doctoral studies.* The deployment would take precedence and I would have to waive the doctoral program, at least for now.

I immediately informed my commander that I was getting out of the military. I said, "Sir, I'm getting out in a year. This is really hard for me, this will be my fourth time deployed in six years overseas, but I know what I signed up for."

I said, "I just feel like I can't get a break. This is turning into my life and I don't have a life anymore, but I'm here to work and will do what you need." I was just honest with him.

He said, "Okay." Then I left.

I went home and prayed about it, but I didn't have the energy to think about it anymore. I knew if I deployed I couldn't pursue my doctorate, because January 14th was the start date, and they wanted me to deploy on December 26th.

In the end, they decided to keep me there. I was so relieved. This allowed me to get settled into the U.S. and get my doctorate. Shortly after, I reconnected with a lieutenant I'd trained in Kentucky in 2014. Her name was Maddy. She told me she was in El Paso near my duty station, and we met up and went to dinner. She helped me move into my place. We talked about so much, including Korea and missile defense (she was in missile defense, so she knew that career path well). At some point in the conversation, I decided to tell her the story about James and the IED.

Nervously, I told her, "I don't know what to do with this…what do I do?"

She simply told me, "You should go tell him."

Kelly had told me I should share the story by writing it down, but Maddy was the first person who told me to go tell James. It had never occurred to me. I wondered, what if things were different, and it was his vehicle that had gotten hit with the IED? What positive impact could this have on him if I told him about the guardian angels I had seen? I wondered, what would he think if I told him?

Despite my reservations, I decided that eventually I had to tell him.

CHAPTER EIGHT
You Can Do All Things Through Christ

After getting out of the military, I often thought back to something that happened when I was in Korea.

It was August of 2017, and I was on vacation in Bali with some friends. I went down to the beach by myself to do some exploring. As I sat with my toes in the sand, staring out at the sea, I noticed a purple seahorse wash up to my feet on the incoming wave. I'm really into animals and I'd never seen a seahorse in real life, outside of an aquarium. So, I freaked out. I thought, *oh my gosh...I have to get you back into the sea so you won't die!*

I cupped my hands around the tiny creature and placed it back in the water. Then I sat down in the sand—and it rolled back up to my feet again! I said, "Oh no! You have to go back." This went on until finally it stopped washing up on the shore and I was sure it was safely back in its home environment.

The whole thing felt like a metaphor for God's forgiveness.

Getting out of the military, I knew I'd be out of my normal structure and routines. I wouldn't be receiving orders to do things, I would have to choose my civilian life and figure out what to do with my time. How many times have I wandered off track? How many times have I messed up? How many times did I do my own thing instead of what I was supposed to do? How many times will I be forgiven? How many second chances has God given me?

God's forgiveness really clicked for me. No matter what you do, God will always love you. No matter who you are, God will love you. That means no matter how far you stray from your purpose, you have to get back on your path, learn from your mistakes and keep moving forward. You have to get back to your goals and get back to living.

As I transitioned out, I knew this was going to be a big step for me (I knew nothing else). It was very important to make sure my priorities were correct, but to be honest, I got sidetracked a little.

The first thing I did was plan a vacation to South America. It sounds crazy now, but as soon as my leave started, I bought a one-way ticket on a cruise to Brazil, Argentina, Chile, Paraguay, Falkland Islands and finally Antarctica (which I never got to because there was a snow delay). I had gotten a certificate to teach English as a foreign language, TEFL, and I thought if I didn't get any job offers in the States, I would pick a country and start teaching English there. I invited a friend to come along with me on the trip, but told him it was my time off and I just wanted to relax. The cruise was my treat to myself.

I ended up getting an offer for a job at Amazon while I was on my vacation, so my dreams of teaching in Brazil didn't pan out, and I bought a ticket back. After arriving in El Paso, I drove up to Denver, Colorado to start my job at Amazon.

It was January of 2020, and this was my very first civilian job. This was interesting timing because the Covid-19 global pandemic hit right after I started. We got extremely busy because people were locked down and shopping more online, and I ended up working overtime constantly. I was coming in on my days off, working longer hours, and I was unable to focus on school. It almost felt like being back in the military (which is ironic because they got rid of PT, the thing I hated most, right after I left).

By September, I realized all I could think about at work was how much I didn't want to be there. I was extremely unhappy. This job was supposed to be something I could do in the interim while I was earning my doctorate, but instead it had become the priority. Meanwhile, my grades were suffering. I had a couple near misses, and I was almost sure I was going to fail three or four classes in my doctorate program. No matter how frustrating it was, no matter how many setbacks, I told myself I had to finish my degree. Even if it takes me six years to do it, I'm still going for it.

Finally, one day I told my bosses, "Hey, this isn't really working out." I wasn't mad at anybody in particular, but I realized it just wasn't what I wanted to do. Working at Amazon was really a good wakeup call on the importance of quality of life. There are more important things in life than work and earning a paycheck.

My uncle gave me some good advice, he said, "Life isn't about making an income, it's about making an impact." You can always make a difference in someone's life, because you never know who is watching you and is encouraged by you. Keeping Christ at the center of my life was important because that's how I could make an impact.

After Amazon, I knew the first thing I had to do was find a job that wouldn't interfere with my school work. I had a couple other job offers with really good pay, but I ended up turning them down because I was afraid the same thing would happen. Finally, I took a job with a company that allowed me to work from home. Immediately my quality of life skyrocketed, I started sleeping more, and I had weekends and time at home. It finally fell into place.

When I left the military the one thing I knew I wanted to do was run for Congress, but I also knew now wasn't the time. So, I kept it in the back of my mind. Adjusting my work schedule allowed me to start writing this book and also pursue another passion of mine, acting and modeling, so I signed with an agency in Denver. My path started to open up and I could start focusing on finishing my degree and running for Congress. My priorities felt like they were finally set, and this allowed me to bring Christ back to the center.

From my perspective, Satan doesn't want good things for you. If you sit there and dwell on your past achievements or your failures, you're going to stall out. If you hesitate, you'll miss your opportunities. I know all things are possible through Christ, and I know, no matter what happens, I need to keep moving.

Praise God.

CHAPTER NINE
Just Look Up

As I was writing this book, I often wondered if anyone was going to believe me. After all, this is my first book and it may only reach one or two people who will be receptive to this message.

These were the exact notes that I wrote down:

"I want this to be a book that can encourage others and let people know that God is always there for them."

There are going to be people who don't believe me, or believe something differently, and that's okay. I wrote this book wanting to share my experience because God put it on my heart to share it. I hope it can help someone in some way. Maybe the people who don't believe are the ones who need to hear it the most, or maybe someone needs to hear this story to help them keep moving on.

For military service members who are out there struggling—you are not alone. For Christians who are being mocked or talked down to, I know how these things feel and it's not fun at all by any means. If this book can make you feel a little bit less alone on your path, then sharing this story will have accomplished something meaningful.

As I came to this last chapter, I could not think of exactly how I wanted to end this book. I came to the conclusion that I simply wanted to let people know that God is always there for them. We often feel we're walking alone and no one is there with us, but that's not true. No matter what you're going through, I want you to know that God is there for you.

Before I left for Afghanistan, I talked with my pastor. It was a bit of a somber discussion, it felt like there was uncertainty. I knew though, no matter what, it would be God's will. Whether I came home or not, God would still be in control. He told me, "Brother Joey (he has known me since I went by Joey), you are as safe here in my office as you are behind a rock in Afghanistan."

That really changed my perspective. It helped me to stop putting God in a box and know that everything that we go through is for a reason. Everything we go through is truly an opportunity. Now, when I feel like I'm going through something difficult, I think, "Why am I going through this and what can I learn from this? What is God trying to teach me?"

As you know from my experiences in this book, I didn't always have someone there personally for me here on Earth. But I always knew that God was right there for me. That is what kept me going.

I have a favorite verse from John 11:42, where Jesus was praying before raising Lazarus from the dead, and he said, "And I knew that thou hearest me always: but because of the people which stand by I said it, that they may believe that thou hast sent me." It didn't matter whether you were behind a rock in Afghanistan, on a mountaintop, or at home, God always hears us and he's always there. If you take away nothing else from this book, I hope you take that with you.

Before I end this chapter, I want to share one final story.

During my military training, I remember I was really struggling. One day we were in the woods and I was carrying a lot of heavy weight, and I just felt like quitting.

I kept thinking, *why am I here? Why am I doing this?*

Just then, I looked up and saw a small opening in the sky through the trees. I remember thinking, *somewhere else, somewhere, things are normal.* People are getting mad at not making a stoplight, people are running stop signs, and people are ordering coffee, and there is normalcy. It's just not like that right here, right now. Right now, I'm going through this, but I know somewhere else it's all okay.

It helped me escape the moment for a second and to keep going knowing that this was just a moment and it too would pass. I just had to get out of that moment and step into another and go somewhere else. I told the people I was with, "If you see me looking up, I'm not daydreaming or hallucinating, it's just helping me concentrate, helping me escape for a moment because I'm really struggling."

When I came home, I never mentioned it again. One day I was talking with one of my close church friends and I remembered this moment, so I told him the story. I'd never really understood it before but immediately he said, "Oh, what a great message!"

"What?" I asked.

"Just look up," he said. "Just look up to God."

I had been thinking about that moment for so long and never had drawn that conclusion, but immediately it made sense. "Just look up." To this day, sometimes I will just stop what I'm doing, and just look up. I look to the sky. At first, it helped me get out of my situation and re-focus. Now, I think, *there is a God, a Savior.* A God that gave his only begotten Son that whosoever believeth in Him should not perish but have everlasting life. It lets me know that no matter what I'm going through no matter where I am, God is there with me.

God knows everything before it happens, but as we continue in life, we do not know what tomorrow brings. I would like to encourage you to continue in the faith. Continue pursuing God's purpose in your life. Continue to pursue your dreams. God is there for you every step of the way, and if He brings you to it, He will bring you through it. For it is written, Hebrews 13:5, "Let your conversation be without covetousness; and be content with such things as ye have: for he hath said, I will never leave thee, nor forsake thee."

We are all facing giants. It can sometimes feel like we're in the valley. Know that you're not alone. When you feel doubt or are unsure of a situation, don't base your action or trust on your strength or what you think you can do. Base it on what you know God can do. For His strength is made perfect in our weakness. For it is written, "I can do all things through Christ which strengtheneth me."

One last thing, I don't want you to think I'm special. I just wanted to share that God is real and God will always be there for you. You don't have to see angels, or feel angels, but there is a very real presence there. Always remember: Just because you can't see something, doesn't mean it isn't there.